Seeds of a Nation

Kentucky

Other titles in the Seeds of a Nation series include:
California
Florida
Illinois
Indiana
Minnesota
New York
Ohio
Texas

Seeds of a Nation

Kentucky

Sheila Wyborny

KIDHAVEN
PRESS™

THOMSON
─────★─────™
GALE

San Diego • Detroit • New York • San Francisco • Cleveland
New Haven, Conn. • Waterville, Maine • London • Munich

© 2003 by KidHaven Press. KidHaven Press is an imprint of The Gale Group, Inc., a division of Thomson Learning, Inc.

KidHaven™ and Thomson Learning™ are trademarks used herein under license.

For more information, contact
KidHaven Press
27500 Drake Rd.
Farmington Hills, MI 48331-3535
Or you can visit our Internet site at http://www.gale.com

LIBRARY OF CONGRESS CATALOGING-IN-PUBLICATION DATA

Wyborny, Sheila, 1950–
Kentucky / by Sheila Wyborny.
  v. cm. — (Seeds of a Nation)
Summary: Discusses the early history of Kentucky from the indigenous Native Americans through exploration and settlement, to statehood in 1792.
Includes bibliographical references and index.
Contents: The land and the first people—Explorers and trailblazers—Settlement and conflict—Struggles for independence and statehood.
  ISBN 0-7377-1446-8 (hardback : alk. paper)
  1. Kentucky—History—To 1792—Juvenile literature. [1. Kentucky—History—To 1782.] I. Title. II. Series.
  F454 .W93 2003
  976.9'01—dc21
                                                                        2002013945

Printed in China

Contents

Chapter One

The Land and the First People

Kentucky gets its name from *Ken-tah-teh*, a Cherokee phrase meaning "tomorrow, the land where we will live." Kentucky is in the central eastern United States. It shares its borders with seven states: Indiana and Ohio to the north, Illinois and Missouri to the west, Tennessee to the south, and West Virginia and Virginia to the east.

The state has six land regions: the Appalachian plateau in the eastern part of the state; the Bluegrass, which gives the state its nickname and occupies the north-central part of the state; the Knobs, which is a small strip around the Bluegrass; the Pennyroyal, which covers most of south-central Kentucky; the Western Coal Field, bordered on the north by the Ohio River;

and the Jackson Purchase, a point of land at the extreme west end of Kentucky.

Kentucky's **landforms** are as **diverse** as its history.

The First Kentuckians

The first people, the **Paleo-Indians,** hunted this region about twelve thousand years ago. They followed herds of mastodons, wooly mammoths, and giant buffalo into the region. They traveled the low hills and grasslands that attracted the large mammals. As they followed the herds, they also gathered edible wild plants.

But the climate began warming and the herds of large mammals, used to a cold climate, died off. To survive, the first people had to hunt deer, turkeys, and other wild game, and catch fish from the rivers. They also had to depend on food from plants. By this time, about three thousand years had passed since the first people arrived.

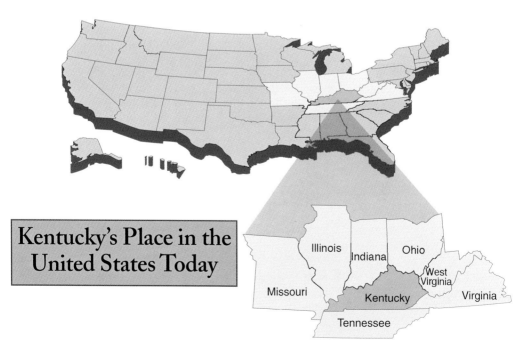

Kentucky's Place in the United States Today

Archaeologists believe that these early people moved in small bands of related families. We know these groups traveled the grasslands because of spear tips that have been found in the grassland areas.

As more time passed, some of these early people constructed cliff dwellings for homes and some built earthen mounds for ceremonies and for burying their dead. Three of these groups were the Hopewells, the Mississippians and the Fort Ancients.

The Hopewell Culture

The earliest of these three groups was the Hopewells. They lived in Kentucky and surrounding areas from about twenty-two hundred to about fifteen hundred years ago. They constructed burial mounds for their dead. Even though the Hopewell existed many years ago, some of these mounds can still be seen today.

The Hopewells made fine jewelry and decorations of copper, mica, and freshwater pearls. Sometimes they used animal teeth and quartz. Many of these ornaments were buried with their dead. The Hopewells also made musical instruments, called panpipes, in the shapes of animals, and made tools from copper.

The Hopewells used obsidian and chert to makes knives, spear points, and arrow points. They also carved animal-shaped tobacco pipes from minerals, and they made clay pottery in many fanciful forms, such as real and imaginary animals. They decorated the pots by painting or pressing fancy designs into them. Archaeologists have found some of these pieces, and they are still in good condition.

A group of Hopewell men perform a cremation ritual.

For food, they hunted, fished, gathered wild edible plants, and farmed.

The Mississippians and the Fort Ancients

The Mississippians appeared a few centuries after the Hopewells. They lived in western Kentucky and survived until about three hundred years ago. This group lived in houses built of pole frames, mud-plastered walls, and thatched roofs. Their villages had a central plaza that was used for dancing, trading, and playing games.

In addition to being good hunters, the Mississippians were successful farmers. They grew sunflowers, squash, corn, and beans. They made picks and hoes to work their crops.

The mounds built by the Mississippians are called temple mounds. These mounds had flat tops, and Mississippian priests lived in homes built on the tops of these mounds. Special ceremonies were held on the mounds' flat tops. Remains of many of the Mississippians' mounds can also be seen today.

Some people in the Mississippian culture developed special skills and crafts, such as making decorative pottery. They made pots and jars in the shapes of animals and carved fancy ornaments from shells. These shells came from freshwater shellfish and were traded with coastal tribes.

The Fort Ancient people lived in Kentucky about the same time as the Mississippians. They were skilled hunters and built large rectangular homes. In excavations, archaeologists have found European tools alongside artifacts of the Fort Ancient people, leading the archaeologists to believe that the Fort Ancients might have been the first Indians in Kentucky with whom European explorers had contact.

But within a hundred years or more before the arrival of the European settlers in Kentucky, these people were mostly gone. It is believed that diseases, brought to this continent by European explorers and settlers, killed the natives. The early people had no natural **immunity** to these diseases. As a result, entire cultures were wiped out. What few Indians survived in this region settled along the Ohio River and other waterways, rather than the uplands and the interior. But even though few Indians actually occupied this land now called Kentucky, by the time the Europeans arrived several groups wanted control over it.

Temple mounds built by the Mississippians between 1000 and 1500 A.D. still exist in Kentucky today.

The Hopewell and Mississippian Indians created fine pottery (pictured) that was often decorated with animal carvings.

Bloody Ground

Although few Indians lived in Kentucky permanently, many wanted the use of the land. They came into Kentucky during hunting season, harvested game, and returned to their homelands. With several different groups wanting to use the land for hunting, land skirmishes occurred between these groups and many were killed.

Some of the tribes who tried to gain control of the land were the Iroquois from New York, the Cherokee and the Chickasaw from the Tennessee valley, the Shawnee, the Wyandottes, and the Delaware from north of the Ohio River. But of these groups, the Shawnee had a greater interest in controlling the Kentucky hunting grounds, because many of them lived permanently in Kentucky.

Making a Stand

The Shawnee had made Kentucky their homeland many years before the arrival of the first Europeans. Because it was Shawnee homeland, they fought for control of Kentucky. The Shawnee had a strong and well-governed society. Both women and men had important roles and responsibilities in the community. Unlike most tribes, women could become chiefs. The women chiefs decided

Kentucky's rich hunting grounds, like the grand Cumberland Gap (pictured), drew several Indian tribes to the region.

when, where, and how the crops would be planted, and they even had the power to stop their warriors from carrying out raids.

The Shawnee were fierce warriors and were willing to fight to the death to hold on to their hunting grounds. They were willing to fight other tribes and anyone else who ventured into their territory. But soon the Shawnee had to fight a new and very different invader, one they knew absolutely nothing about.

Chapter Two

Explorers and Trailblazers

Although Spain claimed all the lands touched by the Mississippi River during the conquistadors' exploration in 1541, they probably never actually visited Kentucky. When three French explorers—René Robert Cavelier Sieur de La Salle, Jacques Marquette, and Louis Jolliet—arrived in the 1670s, they explored and claimed the lands bordering the Ohio River and its tributaries. The French showed more interest in trading with the Indians than in owning their lands, however. The English colonists showed the greatest interest in the lands that came to be known as Kentucky. One of the earliest colonists to risk a trek into this wild but bountiful land was physician and surveyor Dr. Thomas Walker.

Dr. Thomas Walker

Thomas Walker was at one time the physician of Peter Jefferson, Thomas Jefferson's father. After Peter Jefferson's

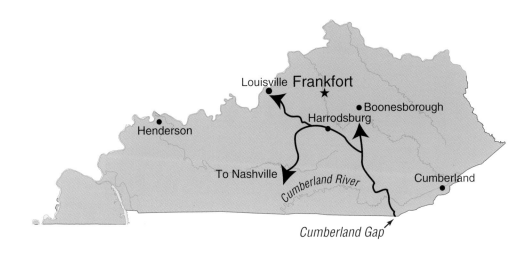

death, Walker became guardian to young Thomas. Walker and his family were quite wealthy and enjoyed a lavish and comfortable life in Virginia. Walker had learned to love exploration, likely from his old friend Peter Jefferson.

Walker earned a reputation as a skilled explorer and surveyor. In 1743 he led a westward expedition to what is now Kingsport, Tennessee. On March 6, 1750, forty-five-year-old Walker and his men set out on what became a four-month expedition. They traveled over the Appalachian Mountains and into the land that came to be known as Kentucky. Walker had been appointed land agent for Loyal Land Company of Virginia, which had an eight hundred thousand-acre tract of land, obtained through a grant in 1748.

While venturing into this wilderness, Walker and his men reached a point called Cave Gap later renamed **Cumberland Gap,** on April 13. Four days later, Walker and his party came to a river. Walker named it the Cumberland River, in honor of the English duke of Cumberland.

For the next week they followed the river farther into the region, but then a horse and one of Walker's men were injured. The accident happened on relatively flat bottom land, so Walker left part of his followers on this site. He instructed them to build a shelter and to plant corn, the two conditions for establishing Loyal Land Company's claim to the land. Walker and the remainder of his group explored farther into the region before returning to the shelter site to organize their party for the return journey to Virginia. Not only had they successfully established claim to the land, but hunting had been plentiful, as well. According to Walker's records, they had shot 13 buffalo, 8 elk, 53 bears, 20 deer, and 150 turkeys.

Word of the Walker party's success reached other adventurers over the years. One of those adventurers was Daniel Boone.

Daniel Boone

In the fall of 1767 Pennsylvania-born Daniel Boone, thirty-two years old, trekked toward the Cumberland Gap from his home in North Carolina. Boone, along with a few companions, intended to hunt and trap, but the hunting party became confused and lost in the dense woods of eastern Kentucky. They returned home in the spring, but Boone was determined to go back to Kentucky for a successful hunt.

In May 1768, Boone, his brother-in-law John Stewart, friend John Finley, and a few followers set out to travel through the Cumberland Gap. They wanted to see the land beyond the Appalachian Mountains with hopes of returning with a wealth of furs. It was two years before Boone's wife, Rebecca, saw her husband again.

Daniel Boone hunted in the Cumberland Gap and later returned as one of Kentucky's earliest white settlers.

Daniel and Squire Boone escape a Shawnee Indian attack (right) while John Stewart (lying on ground) is killed and scalped.

The group hunted through the remainder of the summer and fall, amassing stacks of skins, just as they had hoped. But they were careless and failed to keep lookout for the Indians, who had been using these lands as their hunting grounds for generations. Shawnee hunting parties surrounded them, captured Boone and Stewart, and took their entire supply of skins. Later, the Shawnee released the men, warning them to leave Kentucky and never return. But Boone and Stewart did not heed the warning.

They found the party's campsite and continued their hunt. Often, one of them would leave camp alone to hunt for a day or two. Stewart went off alone one day to hunt and never returned. Boone and the remainder of the party assumed Stewart was killed by Indians. This was an especially sad time for Boone, because in addition to being his brother-in-law, John Stewart was also a good friend.

This hunt continued until March 1771, when the men loaded their horses with hundreds of dollars' worth of animal pelts and headed home to the Yadkin valley in North Carolina. Once again, they were attacked by Indians who took not only the animal pelts, but the horses, as well. They walked home in May, empty-handed.

Even this did not discourage Boone. He was determined to succeed in Kentucky and waited for the opportunity to return to this land of great natural wealth. Two years later, Boone returned to Kentucky once again. This time he built a settlement and brought his wife, eight children, and other settlers.

But someone beat Boone in founding the first settlement in Kentucky. This honor went to James Harrod.

James Harrod

Judge James Harrod was born in Pennsylvania in 1746. Although his role in Kentucky's history is often overlooked, Harrod actually founded the first settlement in Kentucky. People described him as tough and fearless. He was also an excellent hunter.

Harrod had actually begun the settlement in 1774, but it had been abandoned because of the danger of hostile Indians. The following year, he and his men returned to Harrodstown, southwest of present-day Lexington, to finish the job. They finished building the fort and the cabins and planted crops.

Harrod's group also surveyed areas that later became Danville, Big Spring, and Boiling Springs.

As years passed, Harrod became a successful farmer, and he still enjoyed going off by himself to hunt. He would often wander into the deep forests around Harrodstown for days, then return with a load of pelts. In 1825, when he was well into his fifties, Harrod loaded his rifle, ammunition, and supplies for one of his solitary

Replicas of the fort and log cabins built by Judge James Harrod and his men can be seen in present-day Harrodsburg, Kentucky.

hunts. When he did not return after several days, his family feared the worst. Although the townspeople searched for him, no sign of James Harrod was ever seen again. His family assumed that he had been killed by wild animals or Indians.

But Daniel Boone was not far behind James Harrod. Boone established his own settlement. And as white men continued to pour into their traditional hunting grounds, the Indians grew more resentful and more violent.

Chapter Three

Settlement and Conflict

The Native Americans in the area, particularly the Shawnee, had hunted the region for generations. Kentucky was their traditional hunting grounds. As white explorers and settlers streamed into Kentucky in increasing numbers, the Indians saw the effect that hunting for profit was having on wildlife. Because the Indians had to hunt to live, they became fearful for their own survival. And as white settlements grew, violent conflict became more common.

Boonesborough

Daniel Boone had already experienced violence and tragedy in Kentucky, and when he returned there in 1775, he faced even more danger.

Boone was hired by the Transylvania Land Company to blaze a trail into Kentucky and establish a settlement. He was selected for this job because he had already made several trips into the region.

The Transylvania Land Company hired Daniel Boone to establish a colonial settlement in the Cumberland Gap (pictured).

In March 1775, Boone and twenty-nine men began creating a trail across the Cumberland Gap. Settlers and their wagons would be able to follow this trail. But this expedition also met with violence. Two members of his group were killed by Indians.

A few weeks after the establishment of Harrodstown, Boone's men broke ground for their settlement on a two-mile-long parcel of land on the south side of the Kentucky River. Before they could bring their families, the men had to clear the land and build homes. They built rough log cabins in four rows, and then for protection they erected a fortress around the cabins. At first, they called the settlement Fort Boone, but later changed the name to Boonesborough.

Finally, the settlement was ready for families and Boone left to get his wife, Rebecca, and their children. The family arrived in Boonesborough in September 1776. But although the settlement had been made as safe as possible for their families, danger awaited nearby.

On July 14, 1776, Boone's daughter, Jemima, and two of her friends, Betsy and Frances, canoed on the river near Boonesborough. The three girls were captured by a party of Shawnee. As the Shawnee dragged the girls out of the canoe and forced them to walk toward the Indian village some distance away, Betsy, although very frightened, had an idea that helped save herself and her

Daniel Boone and his men (pictured shooting in the background) rescue Jemima Boone and her two friends from their Shawnee captors.

friends. She broke tree branches and tore scraps from her petticoat to leave a trail for rescuers. A short time later, Boone and nine men followed Betsy's trail and rescued the girls. Boone and his men outnumbered the Indians and killed two during the rescue. The rest of the girls' captors escaped into the dense woods.

The girls and all the Boonesborough settlers had learned a lesson about being on their guard at all times. This was only one of many times that Kentucky's settlers faced danger and death.

Fight for Survival

In 1777 nearly every community in Kentucky was raided by Indians. Logan's Station (near present-day Stanford) was under siege for thirteen days. Settlers were near starvation and risked death to go beyond the fort's walls to get milk from the cows. One of the settlers was wounded in his daring attempt and then rescued by several of his neighbors.

In 1778, Boonesborough was attacked by more than four hundred Shawnee. The Indians shot flaming arrows into the fort. Luckily, recent heavy rains protected the roofs from fire. The Indians also tried to dig a tunnel under the walls. Boone made a makeshift cannon from a hollowed-out log and filled the cannon with gunpowder and shot. The first time it was fired, the cannon worked, forcing back the Shawnee. After ten days of relentless assault, the Indians gave up and left. But the battles continued elsewhere.

In October 1782, an isolated cabin near Crab Orchard was invaded by a band of Indians. In the cabin was

Shawnee men (pictured) get ready to spring a surprise attack on the Logan Station settlement.

a male African slave, a white woman, and her two children. After seeing that the cabin was unguarded, one Indian walked right into the cabin and attempted to capture the slave, who was much larger than the Indian. The slave overpowered the Indian, and the mother killed the Indian with an axe. The children shut and barred the door, but several Indians began hacking at it with their tomahawks. The only weapon in the house was a rusted old gun barrel. The mother, knowing she had only one chance to save her family, attempted a bluff. She shoved the gun barrel through a hole in the wall. After seeing the gun and thinking the cabin's inhabitants were going to start shooting, the Indians fled. The mother's desperate bluff had saved her family.

In another isolated spot in Kentucky, Indians attacked the cabin of Mr. and Mrs. John Merrell. Early in the assault, Mr. Merrell was wounded. His wife stood protectively over his unconscious body, swinging an axe. She killed four of the Shawnee before the attackers fled.

Life was difficult and dangerous during the early years of settlement, but the settlers hung on, refusing to give up their new homes.

Life in the Settlement

When more people arrived in a settlement, neighbors worked together to raise a cabin for the new families. A dozen settlers could build a cabin in less than a week. After a cabin was finished, they would have a party with food, music, and dancing to welcome the new families. And although there was no dating, young people had opportunities to spend time with each other.

The settlers knew that the more people living in the settlement, the better chance the settlement had for survival. As a result, everyone worked together for the welfare of the settlement. Many of the settlers were experienced farmers and raised crops to provide food for everyone.

As winter approached, the women gathered supplies to get them through the harsh weather. They spun yarn and wove blankets to protect their families from winter's chill, and they made soap and candles from animal fat.

The men hunted to provide meat for the settlement, and wild game was in abundance. Hunting parties might return to the settlement with black bear, swamp rabbit, river otter, cougar, deer, fox, mink, opossum, raccoons, or

In this oil painting, two men hunt a deer buck in the lush Kentucky river valley.

woodchucks. There were also nearly three hundred species of birds and two hundred varieties of fish. The men were also responsible for defending the settlement when it was attacked. Additionally, men made the laws and governed the people of the community.

The children had important roles in the welfare of the community, as well. Once the men made certain that

Log cabins like this one were built by groups of settlers when a new family arrived at the settlement.

the area was safe from Indian attack, children went to the woods to gather herbs and berries, from which the women made medicine. The children were also responsible for scaring birds and other animals from the gardens.

And so the influx of new settlers into Kentucky continued, and the problems and hardships of settling the wilderness with its abundant resources continued, as well.

Chapter Four

Struggles for Independence and Statehood

To survive in Kentucky, settlers had to endure Indian attacks and deal with the hardships of living in an undeveloped wilderness, completely lacking the conveniences of the cities back East. They also had to help in the battle for independence from England and sometimes had to fight their own government for the land they believed they owned free and clear.

Disputes

By 1776, Transylvania Land Company, the company that had sent Daniel Boone into Kentucky, had more than nine hundred land claims registered as thousands of settlers continued to pour into Kentucky. One major land purchaser was Richard Henderson.

By May 1775, Henderson's company had helped establish four settlements: Boonesborough, Harrodstown, Boiling Springs, and Saint Aspah's Springs (near present-day Stanford). Henderson's plan was that the Transylvania Land Company would govern the region. Henderson and his followers held a convention to set up

Being a skillful hunter helped many men prepare for fighting in the Revolutionary War against England.

their own system of government. When they presented their plan for governing Kentucky to the **Continental Congress** in Philadelphia, which had the power to authorize their plan, the Continental Congress rejected it. Instead, it ruled in favor of Virginia, which claimed that Henderson never had permission from England to set up his company or to enter into treaties with the Indians.

Back in Kentucky, Henderson's land purchasers, too, were in disagreement with the Transylvania Land Company. They had learned that the land they purchased from the land company would have cost less had they bought it directly from Virginia.

One of the disgruntled new Kentuckians was George Rogers Clark. Clark was just as ambitious as Henderson and was determined to break Transylvania Land Company's control over Kentucky. Clark suggested a second convention in Kentucky, and he was selected as one of the delegates. Clark took the new proposal, which connected Kentucky to Virginia, to the Williamsburg, Virginia, assembly. He wanted Virginia to promise its authority over Kentucky. On December 7, 1776, Kentucky was declared a county of Virginia, with Harrodstown as its county seat.

But Clark's plan was not popular with all Kentuckians. Many settlers were angry, charging that Virginia had not provided enough defense during the height of the Indian troubles, nor was Kentucky being protected from British invasions. Virginia attempted to improve the government by making it more regional. To do this,

George Rogers Clark opposed the practices of the Transylvania Land Company and helped make Kentucky a county of Virginia.

Kentucky was divided into three counties, each with its own seat of government. Jefferson County was the land to the west of the Kentucky River, Fayette County to the north, and Lincoln to the south side of the river. But despite Virginia's efforts, Kentuckians were still angry. They claimed that most of the land titles under dispute were decided in favor of the already wealthy native Virginians.

Such disputes continued throughout the period of the Revolutionary War. These problems, along with continuing Indian raids and assaults by the British, added to the hardships of the new Kentuckians.

Sacrifices and Hardship

On July 4, 1776, the American colonies officially declared their separation and independence from England. Representatives from the thirteen colonies signed the Declaration of Independence. In response, England sent troops to put down the rebellion in the colonies.

Many Kentucky men left their families behind to join other colonists in the fight against British and Indian forces.

Most of the battles of the Revolutionary War were fought outside of Kentucky, but many men left their Kentucky homes to fight alongside their fellow patriots in the colonies, leaving their families at the mercies of raiding Indians and British invasion. One of the bloodiest Revolutionary War battles took place near present-day Mount Olivet, Kentucky, and brought more personal tragedy to the Boone family.

Battle of Blue Licks

The Battle of Blue Licks on August 19, 1782, was a complete disaster for the Kentuckians, but it was the last major battle of the Revolutionary War fought in Kentucky.

After a two-day attack on the Kentucky settlement of Bryan's Station near Lexington, the Indians and British retreated, pursued by the Kentuckians, who thought they were chasing beaten enemies out of the territory. But the retreat was a deception.

Two hundred mounted Kentucky militiamen at Licking River clashed with a huge band of Indians led by the British. With the Kentucky militia was Daniel Boone. Knowing that they were outnumbered three to one, Boone urged the Kentuckians not to attack. But the younger, less experienced officers ignored Boone. In less than half an hour, about sixty Kentucky militiamen were dead. Boone escaped by swimming down the river, but sadly his son, twenty-three-year-old Israel Boone, was among the dead.

Because of all the Indian attacks, many settlers became so frightened that they left Kentucky for safer

An illustration shows Daniel Boone struggling with an armed Indian. Boone refused to leave despite threats from Indians and the British.

settlements in the East. But for those who remained, much more controversy and many disputes occurred before Kentucky's future was decided.

The Question of Slavery

Although by 1783 the Revolutionary War was drawing to a close and Americans were free from England's control, some Kentuckians were still not free. Large farms in

Kentucky depended on slave labor to tend the crops, but many people in Kentucky were opposed to slavery.

In 1789 a compromise was reached when Kentucky's leaders decided that already freed **bondsmen** (slaves) would remain free, but for this time in the growth of Kentucky, slavery remained legal.

County, State, or Country

The future of Kentucky was not settled at the end of the Revolutionary War. In fact, several conventions were held before a decision was made about Kentucky's role in the United States. The conventions determined whether Kentucky would continue as a county, be adopted as a

Kentucky became the fifteenth state of the United States in 1792 and Frankfort (pictured) was named its capital city.

state, or become an independent country. Many Kentuckians at this time were small farmers and newcomers, concerned with raising a cabin and getting the first crop harvested before snowfall.

In 1784 the first of ten conventions was held to decide Kentucky's future, and meetings continued over a period of eight years.

But finally, in 1792, Kentucky became the United States's fifteenth state. With its brave, hard-working citizens and abundant natural resources, Kentucky became a great asset to a growing young country.

Facts About Kentucky

State motto: United we stand, divided we fall

State nickname: Bluegrass State

State song: "My Old Kentucky Home"

State capital: Frankfort

State flower: goldenrod

State bird: Kentucky cardinal

State wild animal: gray squirrel

State fish: Kentucky bass

State fossil: brachiopod

State industries: manufacturing automobiles, clothing, and machinery; chemical production; food processing; tobacco; coal mining

Famous Kentuckians of the past and the present: Muhammad Ali, John James Audubon, Kit Carson, Jefferson Davis, Abraham Lincoln, Loretta Lynn, Bill Munroe, Carry Nation, Adlai Stevenson, Zachary Taylor

Glossary

archaeologists: People who investigate artifacts from the past.

bondsman: Another word for a slave.

Continental Congress: The group of delegates who governed the thirteen colonies during the period of the Revolutionary War.

Cumberland Gap: The westernmost portion of the Appalachian Mountains, extending from southwest Virginia to northern Alabama.

diverse: Composed of different or unlike qualities.

immunity: The ability to resist disease.

landforms: Natural features of an area of land.

Paleo-Indians: The earliest American people of Asian origin.

For Further Exploration

Thomas and Virginia Aylesworth, *The Southeast: Georgia, Kentucky, Tennessee.* New York: Chelsea House, 1988. Colorful illustrations, photographs, and maps accompany references to the land, the economy, and the history of these southeastern states.

Dennis Brindell Fradin, *Kentucky.* Chicago: Childrens Press, 1993. A colorfully illustrated history of Kentucky from ancient times to present day.

Patricia Kummer, *Kentucky.* Mankato, MN: Capstone, High/Low Books, 1999. Information about the regions, history, people, and economy of Kentucky is accompanied by color photographs.

Lisa Sita, *Indians of the Northeast: Traditions, History, Legends, and Life.* Milwaukee: Gareth Stevens, 1997. Colorful photographs, paintings, and maps illustrate the lifestyles and history of major Indian groups of the Northeast.

Adam Smith and Katherine Snow-Smith, *A Historical Album of Kentucky.* Brookfield, CT: Millbrook Press, 1995. Colorful pictures illustrate this state history.

R. Conrad Stein, *Kentucky.* Danbury, CT: Childrens Press, 1999. A middle-grade historical, geographical, and economic narrative of Kentucky, with arts and entertainment.

Index

Index

Harrod, James, 20–22
Henderson, Richard,
    32–34
homes
    of Fort Ancients, 10
    of Mississippians, 9–10
    of Paleo-Indians, 8
    of settlers, 28
Hopewells, 8–9
hunting
    by Boone, 17–18, 19–20
    by Harrod, 21–22
    Indian control of land
        and, 12–13, 14
    by Paleo-Indians, 7
    for profit, 23
    by settlers, 29–30

Indians
    control of land for
        hunting and, 12–13, 14
    Revolutionary War and,
        37
    see also specific tribes
Iroquois, 12

Jackson Purchase region, 7
Jefferson, Peter, 15–16
Jefferson, Thomas, 16
Jefferson County, 35

Knobs region, 6

land
    claims by settlers, 32
    grants of, 16–17
    hunting and control of,
        12–13, 14
Lincoln County, 35
location, 6
Logan's Station, 26
Loyal Land Company of
    Virginia, 16–17

Merrell, Mr. and Mrs.
    John, 28
Mississippians, 9–10
mounds
    of Hopewells, 8
    of Mississippians, 10

name, 6
Native Americans
    control of land for
        hunting and, 12–13, 14
    Revolutionary War and,
        37
    see also specific tribes

Paleo-Indians, 7–8
panpipes, 8
Pennyroyal region, 6

Picture Credits

About the Author

Sheila Wyborny and her husband, a broadcast engineer, live in Houston, Texas. They like to spend their spare time flying their Cessna aircraft to interesting weekend locations and adding to their small collection of antiques. Mrs. Wyborny enjoys hearing from students who have read her books.